Samuel French Acting Edition

The Agitators

The Story of Susan B. Anthony and Frederick Douglass

by Mat Smart

SAMUELFRENCH.COM   SAMUELFRENCH.CO.UK

Copyright © 2019 by Mat Smart
All Rights Reserved

THE AGITATORS is fully protected under the copyright laws of the United States of America, the British Commonwealth, including Canada, and all member countries of the Berne Convention for the Protection of Literary and Artistic Works, the Universal Copyright Convention, and/or the World Trade Organization conforming to the Agreement on Trade Related Aspects of Intellectual Property Rights. All rights, including professional and amateur stage productions, recitation, lecturing, public reading, motion picture, radio broadcasting, television and the rights of translation into foreign languages are strictly reserved.

ISBN 978-0-573-70830-5

www.SamuelFrench.com
www.SamuelFrench.co.uk

FOR PRODUCTION ENQUIRIES

UNITED STATES AND CANADA
Info@SamuelFrench.com
1-866-598-8449

UNITED KINGDOM AND EUROPE
Plays@SamuelFrench.co.uk
020-7255-4302

Each title is subject to availability from Samuel French, depending upon country of performance. Please be aware that *THE AGITATORS* may not be licensed by Samuel French in your territory. Professional and amateur producers should contact the nearest Samuel French office or licensing partner to verify availability.

CAUTION: Professional and amateur producers are hereby warned that *THE AGITATORS* is subject to a licensing fee. Publication of this play(s) does not imply availability for performance. Both amateurs and professionals considering a production are strongly advised to apply to Samuel French before starting rehearsals, advertising, or booking a theater. A licensing fee must be paid whether the title(s) is presented for charity or gain and whether or not admission is charged. Professional/Stock licensing fees are quoted upon application to Samuel French.

No one shall make any changes in this title(s) for the purpose of production. No part of this book may be reproduced, stored in a retrieval system, or transmitted in any form, by any means, now known or yet to be invented, including mechanical, electronic, photocopying, recording, videotaping, or otherwise, without the prior written permission of the publisher. No one shall upload this title(s), or part of this title(s), to any social media websites.

For all enquiries regarding motion picture, television, and other media rights, please contact Samuel French.

MUSIC USE NOTE

Licensees are solely responsible for obtaining formal written permission from copyright owners to use copyrighted music in the performance of this play and are strongly cautioned to do so. If no such permission is obtained by the licensee, then the licensee must use only original music that the licensee owns and controls. Licensees are solely responsible and liable for all music clearances and shall indemnify the copyright owners of the play(s) and their licensing agent, Samuel French, against any costs, expenses, losses and liabilities arising from the use of music by licensees. Please contact the appropriate music licensing authority in your territory for the rights to any incidental music.

IMPORTANT BILLING AND CREDIT REQUIREMENTS

If you have obtained performance rights to this title, please refer to your licensing agreement for important billing and credit requirements.

THE AGITATORS premiered at the Geva Theatre Center (Artistic Director, Mark Cuddy; Executive Director, Christopher Mannelli) in Rochester, New York on October 21, 2017. The performance was directed by Logan Vaughn, with scenic design by Jack Magaw, costume design by Jessica Ford, lighting design by Christine Binder, sound design by David Lamont Wilson, and casting by Elissa Myers, CSA and Paul Fouquet, CSA. The composer was Juliette Jones, the dramaturg was Jenni Werner, and the stage manager was Frank Cavallo. The cast was as follows:

SUSAN B. ANTHONY ....Madeleine Lambert
FREDERICK DOUGLASS................................ Cedric Mays

THE AGITATORS was a commission from Geva Theatre Center and the New York State Council on the Arts.

Development of *THE AGITATORS* was supported by a residency and reading at the New Harmony Project.

CHARACTERS

SUSAN B. ANTHONY – (thirties or forties) a white woman
FREDERICK DOUGLASS – (thirties or forties) a black man

SETTING

Rochester, Albany, Boston, New York City, and Washington D.C.

TIME

Act One: 1849 to 1869
Act Two: 1870 to 1895

There is an intermission between Act One and Act Two.

The location, city, and date should be projected at the beginning of each scene.

AUTHOR'S NOTES

Susan B. Anthony was born on February 15, 1820 and died on March 13, 1906. Frederick Douglass' birthdate is unknown, but he is believed to have been born in February of 1818. He died on February 20, 1895.

They most likely met in Rochester in 1849, when Susan was twenty-nine and Frederick was thirty-one. They were friends, allies, and adversaries for the next forty-five years.

The actors playing Susan and Frederick should play in their thirties or forties and seem the same age as one another. As the years go by, the actors should embody their characters' advancing age with subtlety, never straying far from their inexhaustible, youthful spirits.

In production, the theatrical choices should capture the essence of agitation more so than any specific time period. The historical songs called for in the script should be used when noted – however, consider using a mash-up of the original song with contemporary-feeling music. Blur the lines between then and now by employing the ideas of classical, hip hop, and rap. (Please see the Music Use Note on page iii.) Stay away from reverence and historical stuffiness. Get inside the guts of these brilliant, flawed, rebellious social activists.

SPECIAL THANKS

Josh Adams

Segun Akande

Esther Arnold, Lori Birrell, Melinda Wallington, Jessica Lacher-Feldman & the University of Rochester Rare Books and Special Collections

Ro Boddie

McKenna Ceci

Valerie Curtis-Newton

Luticha Doucette

Ann D. Gordon, PhD

Emily Gunyou Halaas

Signe V. Harriday

Deborah L. Hughes & the staff of the National Susan B. Anthony House and Museum

Lea Kemp & Kathryn Murano, Rochester Museum and Science Center

Pepsy Kettavong

Rose O'Keefe

Jay Osborne, Rochester Public Library

Jacqueline Parker

Adanna Paul

Marni Penning

Christine Ridarsky, Rochester City Historian

KenYatta Rogers

Mikell Sapp

Vicki Schmitt & the Friends of Mount Hope Cemetery

Lynn Sherr

John Stauffer, PhD

For Jenni Werner and Logan Vaughn

(In darkness, a breath.)

(In. Out. In.)

(A heart beats. Steady, then faster.)

(Chains drag across a wooden floor.)

(Chains fastened to a post.)

(A whip lashes.)

(It lashes again.)

(Again. Again.)

(Elsewhere, in silhouette, we see a tall, broad-shouldered man with a brilliant mane of hair. He holds a violin.)

(He plays three shorts notes of the same pitch followed by a fourth on a lower pitch. The violin quiets the other noise. He plays the last note louder and louder until it loses tune.)

(He pulls the bow from the strings. The sound of another lash.)

(Another.)

(The sound of the gag, the thumbscrew, the pillory, the Bowie knife.)

(The violence of noise grows louder until it is unbearable.)

(The violinist raises the bow and attacks the strings. He plays a few short, strong intervals. It quiets the other noise.)

(The music from the violin is erratic. It has a melody for a moment, and then the melody disappears.)

(The violence of noise returns, gradually becoming louder than before.)

(The man continues to play the violin along with it.)

(Bloodhounds bark. A pistol fires once. Twice.)

(The heartbeat and breath are deafening.)

(A light rises on a tall woman with a piercing stare, some distance away. She watches the man play violin.)

(The cacophony grows and grows until a string on the violin breaks.)

ACT ONE

The Anthony Family Farm
Rochester, New York
Autumn 1849

(A bright Sunday afternoon. The lawn of the farmhouse.)

*(**FREDERICK DOUGLASS**, thirty-one years old, stands on the inside of a split-rail fence. He stares at his violin and the broken string as though he does not understand what he holds in his hands.)*

(Next to him there is a chair and a tray of food. There is a dish of peach cobbler. It looks cold and untouched.)

*(**SUSAN B. ANTHONY**, twenty-nine years old, watches him.)*

SUSAN. Mr. Douglass?

*(**FREDERICK** doesn't hear her. He takes out a pencil and hurriedly writes something down.)*

(He crosses a word out and writes another.)

(He reads over what he has written as he moves his wrist back and forth. He grimaces in pain. Throughout the play he periodically does this.)

Mr. Douglass?

(Startled, **FREDERICK** *looks at* **SUSAN** *for the first time.)*

I cannot tell you how much I have looked forward to meeting you, Mr. Douglass.

You are one of my father's favorite people in Rochester. There is nothing he loves more than the Sunday afternoons you and your family spend here on our farm.

And I apologize that my teaching in Canajoharie kept me away. It is an honor to finally meet you.

But you have barely said a word all afternoon. Why are you out here by the fence, by yourself, in the far corner of the yard? And why have you not tried the peach cobbler I made?

It is cold now.

What were you playing?

What song was that?

Do you not like peaches?

What did you write down? – a moment ago. You do not have to tell me, of course, but I am curious.

*(***FREDERICK** *hands the scrap of paper to* **SUSAN**.*)*

(She slowly reads.)

"We have to do with the past only as we can make it…"

(She points to a word she cannot make out.)

FREDERICK. "Useful."

SUSAN. "We have to do with the past only as we can make it useful to the present and to the future."

(She closes her eyes and repeats it from memory.)

SUSAN. "We have to do with the past only as we can make it useful to the present and to the future."

> *(She gives the scrap of paper back to* **FREDERICK***.)*

Thank you.

> *(Beat.)*

I could not find good peaches in Canajoharie. Since I resigned my position, I have eaten a dozen peaches a day here. And I am not tired of them yet.

I cannot believe you do not like peaches. I should have made an apple cobbler. Next Sunday, I will –

FREDERICK. Did I say I do not like peaches?

SUSAN. You did not say anything at all.

Do you like peaches?

FREDERICK. Yes.

SUSAN. *(Relieved.)* Oh.

> *(Alarmed.)* Then do you not like cobbler?

>> *(Beat.* **FREDERICK** *looks at her curiously and doesn't answer.)*

I offended you earlier – is that what happened?

I never should have stammered up to you and asked you to sign my copy of your autobiography. I apologize. Did I offend you earlier?

FREDERICK. No.

SUSAN. No?

FREDERICK. No.

SUSAN. Then I think you are being quite rude.

FREDERICK. Rude?

SUSAN. Yes, if I put you off earlier, then I apologize and I quite understand your behavior.

But if I did not put you off, then I should think you are being rather rude.

FREDERICK. You did not put me off earlier.

You are putting me off now.

> *(Beat.)*

I am here, in the far corner of the yard, because this is the best vantage point to watch my children play.

To watch my beautiful wife Anna – with our little Annie swaddled to her chest.

To watch your father and your mother, your brothers and your sisters.

You.

Look at all these abolitionists – young and old.

Look at the miracle of our families all together.

It is a glimpse of what the future of this hateful, hypocritical country could be.

Outside this fence, a black man talking to an unmarried white woman is a death sentence. This conversation – right now – is enough to have me killed.

SUSAN. You are safe here.

FREDERICK. I am welcome here.

But there is nowhere in America that I am safe.

(He looks back at his family in the yard.)

Charles! Down from the –

Charles Remond Douglass! Down from that peach tree! You filthy abolitionist!

Now!

(From across the yard, the sound of children laughing. FREDERICK and SUSAN watch.)

SUSAN. Outside this fence, the fact that I am twenty-nine years old and unmarried is scandalous.

Most women my age have six or seven children by now.

FREDERICK. And why do you not?

SUSAN. Oh, the question everyone must ask me!

Do you too think I am incomplete without a husband and six or seven children?

FREDERICK. It is not an indictment. It is only a question.

SUSAN. As soon as a woman marries, she dissolves into her husband. All of the wages she earns go directly to him. She cannot purchase property. She cannot sign contracts.

And if her husband drinks every night and beats her – she cannot divorce him. She cannot leave him.

Because if she did, she would lose her children and be cast out from society forever.

Her only prospects being prostitution and death.

It is a wonder to me that any woman chooses to marry.

FREDERICK. But what about love?

SUSAN. How do you mean?

FREDERICK. What if you fall in love?

SUSAN. Who is to say I have not fallen in love?

FREDERICK. I meant the general you – not you in particular. Because when one falls in love, sometimes it changes one's thinking.

SUSAN. Well, if and when one falls in love, it should not change one's thinking on the injustices of the institution of marriage.

...If I ever fall in love, it will be with an equal.

FREDERICK. When I first met Anna, I was a slave and she was free.

We were not equals.

She was everything I hoped to become.

(Calling out to Anna.) Anna! You are a vision! – standing there with your violin – I love you!

I have loved you since I first saw you in Baltimore walking down South Caroline Street!

> *(He picks up his violin and plays an impassioned riff.)*

Do you hear how much I love you?

> *(He plays another riff.)*
>
> *(From across the lawn, the sound of Anna playing her violin in response.)*
>
> (**FREDERICK** *listens. He smiles.*)
>
> *(He plays a riff, responding to her music.)*
>
> *(She responds to his.)*

(Together, they play a strange, rapturous duet.)
(They finish with a flourish.)
(From across the yard, there is clapping and a burst of approval.)

I owe everything to you – you beautiful, euphonious woman!

(The children laugh.)

(Quietly, to **SUSAN**, *still looking at Anna.)* I only had the courage to run away because I was running away to Anna.

Twelve days after I escaped, we were married.

Throughout my life, it is women who have taught me how to be the man I am.

(Beat.)

Your father said you recently gave your first public speech in Canajoharie – a speech on temperance.

He said it caused quite an agitation.

SUSAN. Agitation is overstating it. It was more of a...stir.

A gentle stirring really.

FREDERICK. It prompted people to start calling you "The Smartest Woman in Canajoharie."

SUSAN. I am afraid that is not much of a compliment.

*(**FREDERICK** laughs.)*

And more accurately, people called me "The Smartest Woman Who Has Ever Been in Canajoharie."

Sadly, still not much of a compliment.

FREDERICK. Your father beams with pride when he speaks of you.

SUSAN. I do not know why. I am a school teacher who quit her job and moved home.

I have done nothing yet.

FREDERICK. He believes you can become anything you want to become.

...Do you realize how unusual your father is?

SUSAN. He is like many Quaker men.

FREDERICK. No, he is not.

Even though Quaker men say they believe in the equality of the sexes, when it comes to their wife – or daughter – speaking her mind with abandon – their conviction wanes.

It may be 1849, but most men, however enlightened, find the idea of a woman giving a public speech repugnant.

SUSAN. And how do you find it?

FREDERICK. I find it...as vital as oxygen.

It is a pleasure to finally meet you.

(He bows his head. It is regal.)

*(***SUSAN*** bows her head. It is regal as well.)*

Please – sit.

SUSAN. No, thank you.

FREDERICK. Sit for a moment – I insist.

SUSAN. I do not know how to sit.

(Beat.)

May I tell you why I resigned my teaching position in Canajoharie?

(Beat.)

It is because I cannot sleep.

I lie awake at night, my mind racing, my heart pounding – only thinking of one thing:

How do we end slavery? How?

Mr. Douglass, what can I do to help?

I know there are many things that my father – and all of my family – have already tried, but nothing has changed.

What more can we *do*?

It is 1849 – how is this still happening?

I cannot think of anything else.

I cannot sleep.

I –

FREDERICK. So we should end slavery because it keeps you up at night?

SUSAN. That is not what I –

FREDERICK. Why then?

>   *(Beat.)*

When is your birthday?

SUSAN. What?

FREDERICK. When were you born?

SUSAN. February Fifteenth, 1820.

FREDERICK. I do not know mine.

Not the day. Not the year.

Do you keep a record of a horse's birthday? Or a mule?

I did not understand – when I was growing up – why did the white children get to have birthdays and I did not?

Why do you get to have a birthday and I do not?

Answer that. Why?

>   *(**SUSAN** tries to find an answer, but she cannot.)*

Slavery is not an idea to me – it is not a great evil that happens far away in the South that keeps me up at night.

Slavery is what stole the first twenty years of my life.

Why do you get to know your brothers and sisters and I do not?

Because mine are in chains – right now – my sisters and my only brother are in chains right now –

And three million of my brethren.

Has your father ever hit you?

SUSAN. What? – no.

FREDERICK. Has he ever whipped you?

SUSAN. No.

FREDERICK. Has he raped your mother?

SUSAN. Mr. Douglass!

FREDERICK. That is what the white man – my father – did. That is what the white master did to my mother. Over and over.

Slavery steals our bodies away from us.

It is a destroyer of family.

> *(He looks out across the yard at his family.)*

Rosetta was born June the Twenty-Fourth.

Lewis on October Ninth.

Frederick – March Third.

Charles – October Twenty-One.

Annie – March Twenty-Second.

They are why slavery must end.

…What I would give – to have known my mother.

What I would give – to look across the yard on a Sunday afternoon and see her.

> *(They look across the yard at Susan's mother.)*

I only saw my mother but four or five times in my life.

After I was born – she was taken from me and put twelve miles away.

But four or five times, at night, she was able to walk the twelve miles

and lie down with me

and sing me to sleep.

And long before I waked, she would be gone. She had to walk the twelve miles again before daybreak or she would be whipped.

She worked sunup to sundown, walked twelve miles, sang me to sleep, then walked twelve miles back before sunup.

And I – I cannot remember the song.

> *(He hums three short notes of the same pitch followed by a fourth on a lower pitch.)*

It is always just out of reach, just beyond.

But I will find it.

I will find my mother's song.

> *(On his violin he plays the three shorts notes of the same pitch followed by a fourth on a lower pitch. He cannot remember any more.)*
>
> *(He plays the four notes again.)*
>
> *(He plays them again.)*
>
> *(He cannot remember it.)*

SUSAN. What can I do to help?

FREDERICK. There is only one thing to do.

> *(Beat.)*

To agitate.

> *(Beat.)*

Agitate, agitate, agitate.

SUSAN. But agitation alone is not enough.

FREDERICK. Agitation is the spark to the fire of all change.

As long as there is slavery, the Constitution is a sham. It is nothing but a piece of paper with lies and unfulfilled promise.

We must make people angry, make them listen, make them talk.

Nothing changes if people are not talking about it. That must come first.

SUSAN. We need more than words.

FREDERICK. Why is it illegal to teach a slave to read?

Because words can shine light unto injustice like no other force.

If I did not know how to read and write, I never could have escaped slavery.

What can you do?

Use your words as weapons for moral change.

Use the privileged air you breathe to speak out against slavery to everyone you know and everyone you meet.

We need you. We need more of our white brothers and sisters to break their silence.

We need you to speak out in the street

in the counting house

in the prayer meeting

in the conference room

by the fireside

from the pulpit,

but especially at the polls.

Convince your father to vote. It is a crime that he has the right, but never has gone to the polls – not once.

SUSAN. Quakers have no interest in voting.

The government is corrupt. If he votes, he becomes a part of that corruption.

The government wages war. If he votes, he condones that violence.

FREDERICK. But if he votes –

SUSAN. He has no interest in voting. Neither do I.

(Beat.)

FREDERICK. You ask me what you can do.

I say use your words. You say we need more than words.

I say you need to convince your father to vote. You say he will not vote.

Why did you ask for my opinion if you did not want to hear it?

(Beat.)

I hate to tell you, Susan, but white folks have a problem with listening.

And the only thing harder for you to do than to listen to a black man is to hear him.

(Beat.)

A shipwrecked man was cast upon the sands of a faraway beach.

SUSAN. What?

(She bites her lip, upset with herself for so quickly going back to not listening. She tries to listen and hear anew.)

FREDERICK. *(Without missing a beat.)* Days before, when the sailors had set sail, the sea was smooth with a smiling surface.

Only after they were well embarked, did the waves turn to fury and send the ship to destruction and doom.

The one man who lived, upon waking on the sands of this faraway beach, cursed the sea for deceiving him. For destroying his ship. For drowning everyone but him.

Much to the shipwrecked man's surprise, the sea arose and replied:

"Lay not the blame on me, O sailor, but on the winds. By nature, I am as calm and safe as the land itself, but the winds fall upon me with their gusts and gales, and lash me into a fury that is not natural to me."

*(**SUSAN** waits for more, but there isn't more. Beat.)*

SUSAN. Am I the shipwrecked man?

Or are you?

Is my father?

FREDERICK. I am partial to Aesop and his fables. Not only because Aesop was born a slave, or that he was African, or that he gained his freedom with his own cunning and intellect, but because Aesop forces us to think about our own twisting, changing, selfish nature.

SUSAN. What is the wind?

FREDERICK. What is the wind?

(He smiles.)

*(**SUSAN** thinks. She listens for the wind.)*

(She tries to hear it. She tries to see it.)

(She realizes it is going to take some time.)

SUSAN. Will you please try the peach cobbler?

FREDERICK. Fine, yes – I will try it.

> *(He picks up the dish of cobbler. The fork falls from the plate to the ground.)*

SUSAN. I will get you another.

FREDERICK. No need.

> *(He is about to scoop up a piece of cobbler with his hands, but he stops.)*

Wait.

Have you had any?

SUSAN. No. But I am starting to think you never will, Mr. Douglass.

FREDERICK. Stop calling me Mr. Douglass. We are nearly the same age.

SUSAN. What shall I call you then?

FREDERICK. Call me what your mother and father call me.

SUSAN. You are a great and famous man – I cannot call you Fred.

FREDERICK. I am your parents' friend. I am your brothers' and sisters' friend. I am yours as well.

SUSAN. Even though I put you off?

FREDERICK. It is the trait I most desire in my friends.

SUSAN. Frederick.

> *(Beat.)*

Fred. No. Frederick.

> *(**FREDERICK** holds the plate out to her.)*

FREDERICK. Have some.

SUSAN. I will later.

FREDERICK. I insist.

> *(**SUSAN**, using her hands, scoops up some of the cobbler.)*
>
> *(**FREDERICK**, using his hands, scoops up some as well.)*

(At the same time, they eat. They chew in silence.)

Ooo. This is the best cobbler I have ever tasted.

SUSAN. My mother said that is what you told her about her cobbler.

FREDERICK. I did.

But I had not yet had yours.

(They laugh.)

(They look out at each other's families.)

SUSAN. ...Do you believe this can ever be a country for all?

FREDERICK. I hope it can be, but Susan...there are great many people who will do anything in their power to prevent that from happening.

SUSAN. I know.

FREDERICK. You do not know.

And I hope you will never know

the depths of hatred that I have seen man descend to.

SUSAN. Then let us – us women and men – reach for the heights together.

(There is a brilliant burst of light.)

(And a flourish of sound.)

(The moment stops. It burns into their memory.)

(Perhaps we hear violin music with a hip hop beat beneath it.[*])

(This moment should feel like the past and the present colliding as one.)

(After several moments, we hear the sounds of an angry mob.)

---

*A license to produce *The Agitators* does not include a performance license for any third-party or copyrighted music. Licensees should create an original composition or use music in the public domain. For further information, please see Music Use Note on page 3.

Association Hall
Anti-Slavery Society Meeting
Albany, New York
February 5, 1861

(It is ten and a half years later.)

(Evening.)

(Smoke is everywhere.)

(There is the pulsing sound of feet stomping, fists pounding walls, and a mob shouting: "Damn the abolitionists! Damn the abolitionists! Damn the abolitionists!")

*(**SUSAN**, now forty years old, and **FREDERICK**, now forty-two years old, rush through a wooden door.)*

(They slam it shut behind them and lock it.)

(They are in a small storage room to the side of the stage.)

(They cough. They cover their mouths with handkerchiefs.)

SUSAN. What happened?

FREDERICK. Someone threw pepper in the stove.

(The sound of the mob on the other side of the door grows louder.)

*(**FREDERICK** takes off his jacket and waves it in the air, trying to get the smoke to dissipate. **SUSAN** fans the air with her handkerchief.)*

(Blood runs from her lip and onto her chin.)

Your lip is bleeding.

SUSAN. It happened when the mob slammed into us.

FREDERICK. We need to get you a doctor.

SUSAN. It is nothing.

(She wipes away the blood with the handkerchief.)

FREDERICK. When your father finds out how I have put you in harm's way –

SUSAN. I am forty years old. I do not answer to my father.

FREDERICK. Yes, but –

SUSAN. You are in danger tonight, same as I.

FREDERICK. But this is my fault for dragging you into this.

SUSAN. I chose to accept this position with the Anti-Slavery Society.

(There is pounding on the door. **FREDERICK** *double-checks the lock.)*

FREDERICK. Need I remind you that last night in Syracuse, they dragged an effigy of you through the streets and then set it on fire?

SUSAN. Better it than me.

FREDERICK. They have bricks and knives and guns.

SUSAN. Mayor Thacher has promised to sit on the stage with us – with a loaded revolver in his lap. He will keep the order.

FREDERICK. But what if he must use it? Are you prepared to condone that violence? To cast aside your Quaker beliefs?

SUSAN. This fight takes precedence.

(A glass bottle breaks against the other side of the door.)

FREDERICK. This is madness – we cannot speak tonight. As soon as Elizabeth and Lucretia arrive, we must all leave out the back.

SUSAN. I cannot believe my ears.

FREDERICK. This feels no different than a mob I spoke to in Indiana.
They threw rocks at me. One gashed me here –

(He touches his temple.)

– and even though blood covered my face, I spoke on.

They overtook the platform. They beat me. They shattered my wrist and knocked me unconscious. They only stopped because they thought I was dead.

(He moves his wrist back and forth.)

SUSAN. Why did you speak on?

FREDERICK. Because I was a fool.

SUSAN. Or was it because you refused to be silenced?

There are men out there who have never heard a woman speak in public. Or a black man. If we can change the mind of *one* of those –

FREDERICK. It is not safe.

SUSAN. No, it is not.

But there must be no union with the slaveholders.

We must convince as many people in the North as we can, as fast as we can.

"Those who profess to favor freedom and yet deprecate –"

FREDERICK. Do not quote me to me.

(Elsewhere in the hall, there is a gunshot.)

*(**SUSAN** and **FREDERICK** drop to the floor.)*

(Another gunshot.)

(The crowd quiets.)

(Another gunshot.)

(Silence.)

SUSAN. I am willing to die for this.

I am willing to die to end slavery in this country.

Are you?

FREDERICK. I answered that question long ago.

(They look at one another – bonded together anew in this fight, bonded together by blood.)

(They stand up. They straighten their clothes.)

*(**SUSAN** wipes a bit of blood from her lip.)*

(Quietly at first, and by the end, afire.) "Those who profess to favor freedom and yet deprecate agitation, are people who want crops without plowing the ground.

They want rain without thunder and lightning.

They want the ocean without the roar of its many waters.

The struggle may be a moral one, or it may be a physical one, or it may be both. But it will be a struggle."

FREDERICK & SUSAN. "Power concedes nothing without a demand. It never did and it never will."

> *(They unlock the door and charge through it together.)*

The Douglass House
South Avenue, Rochester, New York
April 28, 1861

SUSAN. I thought I heard something.

Did you not hear something?

> *(It is nearly three months later. Night.)*
>
> *(**SUSAN** and **FREDERICK** stand in the open doorway. It is silent – except for the wind and an occasional cricket chirp.)*
>
> *(They look up and down the road.)*

FREDERICK. I thought I heard footsteps.

SUSAN. As did I.

> *(They listen. It is silent except for the wind.)*

How can it be so quiet? We are at war now, how can it be quiet?

> *(They listen.)*

FREDERICK. ...Every morning I open the newspaper, new and damp from the press, I am afraid it will say that the Capital has fallen.

SUSAN. I have not slept in the two weeks since Fort Sumter.

FREDERICK. Will your brothers fight?

SUSAN. It is against our Quaker beliefs, but yes, Daniel and Merritt will fight.

My whole family supports their decision.
But I dread the...not knowing
that will come with it.
When Merritt fought with John Brown in Osawatomie
five years ago, the weeks we waited – not knowing if he
was alive or dead – were unbearable.
...Will your sons enlist? – if they are ever allowed to?

FREDERICK. They will be the first in line.
Let the black man get upon his person the brass letters
"U.S."
Let him get an eagle on his button
a musket on his shoulder
bullets in his pockets
and there is no power on earth which can deny that he
has earned the right of citizenship in the United States.

(Beat.)

Was that something?

(They listen.)

It must have been the wind.

(They listen. It is quiet.)

Feels like rain in the air.

SUSAN. Do you think Harriet will have news?

FREDERICK. When has Harriet Tubman ever *not* had news?

SUSAN. Indeed.

(There is thunder in the distance.)

Let us set out the blankets.

FREDERICK. No, if it storms, I do not want you caught out in it. Go home. We can take them all.

SUSAN. No, my family has vowed to take half. I will wait until they arrive and then escort them to our farm.

FREDERICK. Yes, but –

SUSAN. We already have the blankets set out in our living room.
Let us set them out here, too.

(A crash of thunder. It starts to rain.)

(They come back inside the house and close the door.)

*(**SUSAN** goes to a stack of folded blankets that rests on top of a wooden file cabinet.)*

(She begins unfolding the blankets lengthwise on the floor, one by one.)

FREDERICK. What a feast Anna has made for them.

SUSAN. I tried to get here earlier. I wanted to help her cook.

FREDERICK. She is used to it.

(Beat.)

SUSAN. When I arrived, she barely could keep her eyes open and yet I had to plead with her to go to bed. She said she baked twenty loaves of bread today.

FREDERICK. She wants there to be enough for them to take along tomorrow to Canada.

SUSAN. And how many loaves of bread did you bake today?

FREDERICK. Come again?

SUSAN. Do you know how to make bread?

FREDERICK. Why would I make bread?

SUSAN. Perhaps your wife would welcome the help.

(She hands him a blanket.)

(After a moment, he begins helping her set out the blankets.)

(He goes to the bookshelf and hands her a book.)

Madame Bovary.

*(**SUSAN** puts the book at the top of the blanket – to be used as a pillow. **FREDERICK** takes another book from the shelf.)*

FREDERICK. Aesop's Fables.

(There is a long silence as they continue to fold out the blankets, one by one, all over the

floor. They place books at the top of each for pillows.)

*(**FREDERICK** takes another book from the shelf and hands it to **SUSAN**.)*

SUSAN. *David Copperfield.*

*(**FREDERICK** opens the book to the title page.)*

Is this what it looks like?

FREDERICK. When I was in England last year, he attended one of my lectures.

SUSAN. *(Reading.)* "With admiration to Fred Douglass. Your fellow man of letters – Charles Dickens."
What was he like?

FREDERICK. He was in a hurry.
And he had breadcrumbs in his goatee.
That is all I remember.

SUSAN. We cannot put this one out.

(She goes to return it to the shelf.)

FREDERICK. No, please – leave it.
I may not be able to bake bread, but at least I can provide a pillow that is signed by Charles Dickens.

*(**SUSAN** puts the book down as a pillow.)*

*(**FREDERICK** takes another book from the shelf.)*

Robbie Burns.

(They continue to arrange the blankets and books.)

…I have decided on September Third.
For my birthday.

SUSAN. The day you escaped.

FREDERICK. The day I escaped.
…How I loathe that this has become routine.
We are helping human beings
from bondage
to freedom.

It is a sacred act and yet,
it is routine for us.

SUSAN. ...Lord –
Please protect Harriet and our friends.
Please let them travel here unimpeded and unassailed...
Let them find their way to us
with the ease of a shuttle flying in the loom of a weaver.
Amen.

FREDERICK. Amen.

(He hums the first four notes of the song from the beginning. He hums them again but does not continue.)

SUSAN. You still do not remember it?

FREDERICK. No. But I will find it.

(He hums the four notes again but cannot remember more.)

SUSAN. ...I will check on the water.

FREDERICK. No, I will. I, at least, know how to check if a tub of water is warm or not.

(He exits to the kitchen.)

(By now there are five or six makeshift beds on the floor.)

*(**SUSAN** goes to the blankets Frederick set out.)*

(They are somewhat rumpled.)

(She straightens them.)

*(**FREDERICK** re-enters. He has a towel over his shoulder and he carries a wash bin full of steaming hot water. He puts the bin down by a chair.)*

*(**SUSAN** sits down and starts taking off her boots and stockings.)*

(It is the first time we have seen her sit.)

Ladies and gentlemen, Susan Anthony has sat down.

SUSAN. Shush.

...My feet are throbbing.

FREDERICK. My wrist as well.

It never healed correctly. Every time I write, it feels as though it is on fire.

> (**SUSAN** *continues taking off her boots. Perhaps* **FREDERICK** *helps her.*)

SUSAN. ...I am using the B now – in my name.

FREDERICK. Susan B. Anthony?

SUSAN. Yes.

FREDERICK. That will take some time to get used to.

> (**SUSAN** *puts her feet into the hot water.*)

SUSAN. Oh. Heavenly.

> (**FREDERICK** *sits on the floor next to her and puts his bad wrist in the hot water.*)

FREDERICK. Mm-hm. Yes, please, and thank you.

SUSAN. I still do not know how you bear to do that alongside my feet.

FREDERICK. Oh, I have smelled much worse than yours.

SUSAN. Thank you?

> *(They laugh.)*
>
> *(They close their eyes and enjoy the relief of the hot water.)*
>
> *(A long silence.)*

What a fool I was – to be so reckless in the winter of '55 – when I petitioned for married women's property rights.

Why did I think it was a good idea to go to every county in New York in the dead of winter?

It is only luck that the frostbite did not claim any of my toes. Or worse.

But still, my feet are wrecked. And for what?

I was the shipwrecked sailor, shouting at the sea.

Yelling at the sea of fat, white men in Albany about property rights and temperance.

But the sea does not move on its own.

It is moved by the wind.

And the wind is the vote.

It was lunacy to think they would listen to anyone without the power to vote them out of office.

Even my father has finally come around.

FREDERICK. Abraham Lincoln got that Quaker to the polls.

SUSAN. You and I had something to do with that as well.

FREDERICK. True.

SUSAN. I try to imagine it sometimes.

What it will feel like to have a voice.

Imagine the North victorious.

Slavery abolished.

FREDERICK. Amen.

SUSAN. Amen.

Imagine: all of us – all women and men – every shade, every color.

All of us, together, enfranchised.

FREDERICK. Amen.

SUSAN. Amen.

Let us go together – the first time we vote.

Let us stand next to each other as we cast our first ballots – shall we?

FREDERICK. We shall. What a glorious day that will be.

(He moves his wrist in the water.)

*(**SUSAN** moves her feet.)*

"Fight for my rights, Aunt Susan."

Remember when little Annie said that to you?

SUSAN. Yes.

FREDERICK. "Fight for my rights."

...It was a year last month. A year our Annie is gone.

She would have been twelve.

I think of her every day.

> *(They sit in silence for a moment.)*

Do you know how to ice skate?

SUSAN. ...Yes. Why?

FREDERICK. She always wanted to go ice skating on the Genesee River.

Every winter – every time it was cold enough to freeze – she begged us.

We never took her.

Anna and I did not know how to ice skate.

But why did we not learn?

Why did we not buy her skates and take her?

> *(They listen.)*

Do you hear something?

> *(**SUSAN** does not hear anything. She watches **FREDERICK**.)*

Dammit – where are they?

Why aren't they here yet?

Let us speak of something else. No good will come from our worrying.

Tell me a joke.

SUSAN. I do not know any jokes.

FREDERICK. Surely, you must.

SUSAN. ...I know an April joke. Shall I tell it? – since it is April.

FREDERICK. Please.

SUSAN. Why was the soldier so tired in April?

> *(Beat.)*

Because he just had a March of thirty-one days.

> *(**FREDERICK** doesn't laugh. **SUSAN** doesn't either.)*
>
> *(Beat.)*

A thief broke into a lawyer's house.

But you need not worry,

after a *terrible* struggle
the lawyer succeeded in robbing the thief.

> *(Neither **FREDERICK** or **SUSAN** laugh.)*
>
> *(Beat.)*

FREDERICK. …Two scholars had a heated argument about who was smarter.
One of the scholars yelled, "I bet you do not even know the Latin word for goose."
And the other scholar stopped short and thought and thought
and eventually he said, "Alas, I do not know the answer."

> *(He laughs. **SUSAN** does not.)*

SUSAN. I do not understand.

FREDERICK. "Alas, I do not know the *answer*."

SUSAN. What?

FREDERICK. Anser is Latin for goose.

> *(Beat.)*

SUSAN. We are not funny.

FREDERICK. We are hilarious.

SUSAN. Uh…

FREDERICK. How about a story then? Tell me a story.
Take our minds far away from here.

> *(**SUSAN** looks at the water.)*
>
> *(She moves her feet.)*

SUSAN. …On the days that my feet especially hurt, you know what I think of?
How my life would be different if I had accepted the hot plank man's proposal.

FREDERICK. What now?

SUSAN. Have I never told you about my hot plank man?

FREDERICK. No.

SUSAN. He proposed to me. During that terrible winter six years ago.

FREDERICK. Proposed what?

SUSAN. Marriage.

FREDERICK. Is that so?

SUSAN. Do not act so surprised. I have received many marriage proposals over the years.

...I forget if it was Schenectady or Johnstown, but it was a bitterly cold night.

The lecture hall was freezing. The gas lighting was out.

And right before I was to speak he appeared – like a bearded angel – with a steaming thick plank, baked delightfully hot.

He put it under my feet – right there on the stage – and it felt like a little plank of heaven.

Throughout the evening, he brought me hot cups of tea.

The next day he appeared with his sleigh pulled by two beautiful gray mares.

And again – the hot plank – right there in the sleigh for under my feet.

This went on for several days and he was a proper gentleman. He was a perfectly adequate conversationalist.

But finally, unable to stop himself, he blurted out:

"Please, Susan, leave this terrible life you are living and marry me. I shall share with you my heart, my home, and my hot plank forever."

FREDERICK. He did not.

SUSAN. He did.

I told him I was flattered,

but the life I was living was the only one I found endurable.

And then he howled:

"Oh, modern woman! Modern woman is beyond any ordinary man's comprehension!"

And off he went.

Taking his hot plank with him.

Forever.

*(***FREDERICK** *laughs.* **SUSAN** *does not.)*

(She takes her feet out of the basin.)

FREDERICK. You have barely let your feet soak.

SUSAN. I have been sitting long enough.

(She begins to dry her feet. Eventually she puts on her stockings and boots.)

FREDERICK. Now I am curious – how many marriage proposals have you received?

SUSAN. Do not make me regret telling you.

FREDERICK. Is it more or less than ten?

SUSAN. Shush.

FREDERICK. Fifteen?

(Beat.)

Twenty?

(Beat.)

More than twenty?

*(**SUSAN** turns away.)*

So it is more than twenty.

*(**SUSAN** smiles to herself.)*

I am impressed, Susan *B*. Anthony.

SUSAN. I am forty-one years old now.
The proposals have stopped.

FREDERICK. We could try to find your hot plank man.

(Pause.)

SUSAN. I will never be a mother.

(Pause.)

FREDERICK. I did not know you wanted to be.

SUSAN. It is not that I did not want to be a mother. It is that I was unwilling to sacrifice my whole life and everything I am fighting for to do so.

(Beat.)

Why can Anna barely read?

(Beat.)

SUSAN. There is no American more gifted with words than you – you are admired by Charles Dickens himself – and yet your wife cannot read.

I do not understand it.

All of your children can read. Why not Anna?

(Beat.)

FREDERICK. I hired her a tutor once.

Anna sent her packing after one day.

She does not want to learn.

SUSAN. Or does she not have the time to learn?

When I arrived tonight, Anna was ready to fall over in the kitchen and you were reading the newspaper with your feet up. Do you believe her sole purpose is to cook and wash and raise your children while you are away lecturing?

FREDERICK. There is nothing, in this world, more important than raising children.

SUSAN. So when your children were infants, did you change their cotton gowns and diapers?

(Beat.)

If Anna needed to go to a convention – like you so often do – would you mind the children for a week? For a month? For a year?

How is Anna any different than your maid?

FREDERICK. Careful.

SUSAN. I do not understand.

On the platform, you say women have no greater champion than Frederick Douglass, but here on South Avenue, behind closed doors, do you believe something else?

FREDERICK. Anna has her role. I have mine. Both are equally important.

SUSAN. And *that*, Frederick, is why I had to choose between leading this fight and being a mother. These *roles* made it impossible for me to do both.

If ever a man said to me:

"Let us work together in this great cause.

Let me be your companion and aide
for I admire you more than any woman I have ever admired.
Let us be partners
in this great fight.
Let us be equals
outside the home
and within it."
If ever a man proposed that to me, then I would be married.
But no man ever did.
And I wonder if any man
has ever
proposed that to any woman.

> *(In the distance, a low rumbling. The floor begins to shake.)*
>
> *(It is as though the sound is coming from underground.)*
>
> *(**SUSAN** and **FREDERICK** do not seem to hear it.)*
>
> *(The rumbling grows louder and louder.)*
>
> *(The floors and walls shake.)*
>
> *(A train whistle blows.)*
>
> *(The sound of the massive engine of a locomotive.)*

Boston & Maine Railroad Station
Haymarket Square
Boston, Massachusetts
December 10, 1867

> *(It is six and a half years later.)*
>
> *(There are numerous platforms and railroad tracks crisscrossing every which way. It is a bustling train station. The sounds of trains*

and steam fill the air. **FREDERICK**, *now forty-nine, rushes across a platform.)*

SUSAN. *(From offstage.)* Frederick!
Frederick Douglass!

(**FREDERICK** *stops and looks around. He does not see where the voice is coming from.)*

Frederick Augustus Washington Bailey!

(Late for his train and unable to see who is calling him, **FREDERICK** *continues down the platform.)*

(**SUSAN**, *now forty-seven, rushes onto a parallel platform.)*

Frederick!

(She takes a newspaper and throws it at **FREDERICK**.*)*

Fred!

(Hitting him with the paper or not, **FREDERICK** *finally sees* **SUSAN**.*)*

FREDERICK. Hallo there, Friend Susan!

(Throughout the entire scene they must shout to be heard by each other.)

SUSAN. Where are you off to?
FREDERICK. Westborough. And you?
SUSAN. Hartford. How long have you been in Boston?
FREDERICK. What?
SUSAN. What are you doing in Boston?
FREDERICK. What?
SUSAN. I will come over.

(She steps down onto the tracks.)

FREDERICK. It is not safe to cross the tracks!
SUSAN. I am not afraid of trains.

(The rumbling of a train approaching.)

(**SUSAN** *retreats back to her platform.*)
(*The sound is deafening.*)
(*They wait for it to pass.*)

I will use the stairs.

FREDERICK. Are you with George Francis Train?

SUSAN. Yes, and Elizabeth. They are minutes behind me. We lectured here last night.
Hartford is tonight. Where does your train terminate?

FREDERICK. Albany.

SUSAN. I will change my ticket and go with you to Westborough, then transfer to the New Haven line in Springfield.

FREDERICK. It is about to depart –

SUSAN. But we have much to discuss.

FREDERICK. I know – and I apologize I have not yet answered your letters – but this lecture tour has been grueling.

SUSAN. (*Finally saying what she has wanted to say.*) We needed you in Kansas. We needed you and you knew we did.

FREDERICK. This is not a conversation for a train station.

SUSAN. If we had had the full backing of the AERA in Kansas – if you had not let Wendell Phillips cut off our funding –

FREDERICK. I have no say in funding.

SUSAN. If you had come with us, your voice would have made the difference.

FREDERICK. My voice was needed here, too. I cannot be two places at once.

(*He starts to exit.* **SUSAN** *follows him from the parallel platform.*)

SUSAN. Stop! You owe me thirty seconds!

(**FREDERICK** *stops.*)

This country is being reconstructed – as we speak. People are ready for change.

All blacks – all women – together. Equal Rights for All.
We could have passed both referendums in Kansas if –

FREDERICK. Both were soundly defeated –

SUSAN. Because the Republicans betrayed us!
We had no support – no money –

FREDERICK. Is that why you turned to a racist for funding?
George Francis Train is a racist and a bigot. "Women first and the Negro last" – that is his slogan. Why are you and Elizabeth lecturing with him?

SUSAN. He supports woman suffrage. He does not speak of anything else with us.

FREDERICK. Susan –

SUSAN. He offered the money when no one else would.

FREDERICK. He is an insult to everything we are trying to achieve.

SUSAN. "I would unite with anybody to do right and with nobody to do wrong."

FREDERICK. Do not quote me to me.

SUSAN. You are funded by sexists.
You are funded by misogynists.

(**FREDERICK** *takes a breath and is about to respond to this, but stops himself. Beat.*)

FREDERICK. I must go.

SUSAN. Elizabeth and I were crossing Kansas in wagons, fording streams, giving speeches in saw mills.
Our lives were threatened. We were terrified at night. The chance of bandits robbing or raping or killing us was real.
Never was I so driven by desperation.

FREDERICK. Did anything happen?

SUSAN. No. But it is a miracle that nothing did.

(*A train whistles.*)

Let me change my ticket and ride with you to Westborough.

FREDERICK. There is not time.

> *(He rushes down the platform and boards his train just as it departs. Its engines rev. The whistle blasts. The train leaves the station. They look at one another – as the distance grows between them.)*
>
> *(**SUSAN**, now alone, remains on her platform.)*

A Boarding House
New York City
May 12, 1869

> *(It is a year and a half later.)*
>
> *(The foyer of a boarding house. In the middle of the floor there is a large wooden trunk. **SUSAN** kneels on the floor in the middle of a mess of boxes, programs, pamphlets, and papers.)*
>
> *(She sorts through the materials and puts what she needs into the trunk.)*
>
> *(After some time, **FREDERICK** enters.)*

FREDERICK. How have you been?

SUSAN. *(Startled.)* Oh, I –

Busy. And you?

FREDERICK. The same. I arrived at Steinway Hall early for the evening session, but I could not find you. I thought I would check here.

> *(**SUSAN** continues to throw papers and pamphlets into the trunk.)*

SUSAN. I sent the materials here to the boarding house in advance and I did not leave enough time to sort through them. I already should be at the Hall. Elizabeth is probably throwing a fit.

FREDERICK. How can I help?

SUSAN. Anything you see marked for today, put in the trunk.

> (**FREDERICK** *kneels and starts helping with the materials.*)

Thank you.

It is good to see you, my friend.

FREDERICK. And you.

> (*They pack the trunk in silence for a few moments.*)

How long have we known each other now?

SUSAN. Twenty years.

FREDERICK. Hard to believe we have put up with each other for twenty years.

SUSAN. Indeed.

FREDERICK. Feels like at least thirty.

> (*Beat.*)

Tonight, I am going to introduce a resolution that calls for the American Equal Rights Association to give its unequivocal support to the Fifteenth Amendment.

> (**SUSAN** *stops. It is as though she has been punched in the stomach.*)

SUSAN. I... I do not understand.

This is the American Equal Rights Association. Our sole purpose is to secure universal suffrage.

It is not the Black Men's Rights Association.

Nor is it the Women's Rights Association.

It is the *American Equal Rights Association*.

FREDERICK. Yes, but –

SUSAN. The Fifteenth is a constitutional amendment that disenfranchises *half* of this country.

It is the opposite of our mission.

I do not even know what to say to such a despicable suggestion – what shall you have me say?

FREDERICK. That you will stand with me.

(**SUSAN** *cannot believe her ears. Beat.*)

Will you stand with me?

SUSAN. You cannot be serious.

FREDERICK. This in-fighting of the AERA has hurt the chances of the Fifteenth being ratified. It has already been two months and we only have thirteen states. We barely won New York and we still need fifteen more?

If Susan B. Anthony had a change of heart and supported it – that could sway the country.

SUSAN. You overstate my influence.

FREDERICK. You are on the front page of the newspaper once a week. What you say matters.

SUSAN. What I say is *reported* on, but what does it matter without the vote?

FREDERICK. We need fifteen more states to get the Fifteenth ratified – to make the Constitution a little less fraudulent than it is now. We need you.

SUSAN. I will support it with the addition of one word.

"The right of citizens of the United States to vote shall not be denied or abridged on account of race, color, previous condition of servitude or *sex*" –

That one word will make this country whole.

FREDERICK. We tried for it, but –

SUSAN. I tried. You did not.

FREDERICK. We all tried and we all failed – the states are already voting on it. It is too late to change a single word. And if we continue this feud, the AERA will be ripped apart and the ratification of the Fifteenth will be thrown into further jeopardy.

SUSAN. Surely, you know what strings to pull in Congress to make it happen – and with your crony Ulysses in the White House intimidating legislators like he's still on the battlefield –

FREDERICK. He is not my crony.

SUSAN. Oh, that is right, how could he be? He failed to come through with a cabinet appointment for you. Take him off the list!

FREDERICK. After 250 years of bondage, the vote is within reach of the black man – we must take it.

SUSAN. We women stood beside you throughout the Civil War. We put aside our needs because the need to end slavery was greater.

FREDERICK. And we are beyond grateful.

SUSAN. You could not have done it without us!

And now you want to leave us behind?

The wording of the amendment is vague and flawed. It states that the right to vote "shall not be denied or abridged." Why does it not *protect* the right?

You have been in politics longer than I. You know when someone says, "It shall not be denied or abridged," the first order of business will be denying and abridging.

FREDERICK. It is the language we could get.

SUSAN. The Southern States are already plotting ways they could use the amendment to deny and abridge the black man's vote.

FREDERICK. It is what we could get.

It is a step in the right direction.

Please – will you join me?

   (Beat.)

An oak tree that grew on the bank of a river was uprooted by a storm.

SUSAN. I am not in the mood for fables.

FREDERICK. The oak tree was thrown through the air and fell among some reeds growing by the water. It said to the reeds, "How is it that you, who are so frail and slender, have managed to weather the storm, whereas I, with all my strength, have been torn up by the roots and hurled into the river?"

"You were stubborn," said the reeds. "You fought against the storm, which proved stronger than you. But we reeds bow and yield to every breeze, and thus the gale passed harmlessly over our heads."

(Beat.)

Will you be the reeds today?

(Beat.)

SUSAN. No.

(She throws the rest of her papers into the trunk and slams it shut.)

(Calling out.) Porter!

(To **FREDERICK**.*)* I must get to Steinway Hall. I am already late.

FREDERICK. Your support would mean success.

SUSAN. The only thing it would mean is that I, like you, have sacrificed my ideals.
(Calling out.) Porter!

(She puts all of her strength into moving the trunk. It does not move.)

FREDERICK. Let me help you.

SUSAN. I do not need your help!

(She pulls harder on the trunk, but it still doesn't move. She falls to the ground.)

*(***FREDERICK** *offers her his hand. She doesn't take it. She stands on her own.)*

(Beat.)

*(***FREDERICK** *tries to pick up the trunk. It barely moves.)*

(He bends his wrist awkwardly. He grimaces and moves it back and forth.)

FREDERICK. You have overloaded it.
Let us take some out. We can make two trips.

SUSAN. No.

FREDERICK. Sometimes you cannot put everything in at once. Sometimes you have to take it piece by piece.

SUSAN. If I must take it piece by piece, I would first give it to women.

    (Beat.)

What happened?

Up until Kansas, it felt as though we were all in lockstep together.

You and me – Elizabeth and Lucretia – Lucy and Martha and Gerrit – it felt like we all believed we could remake this country together.

When did you stop believing we could pass universal suffrage?

FREDERICK. I still believe.

SUSAN. You would not do this if you did.

FREDERICK. Susan, the men of this country – the men who vote and the men in Congress – are not ready for woman suffrage.

SUSAN. Was the country ready to abolish slavery? Or for a civil war?

How can you know if it is ready for the black man to vote but not women?

FREDERICK. What if we try for both and get neither?

SUSAN. So be it.

    (Calling out.) Porter, please!

Porter!

Move along, Mr. Douglass. The only thing to see here is the carcass of the equal rights movement.

FREDERICK. Come, now.

SUSAN. Do you see me as lesser?

FREDERICK. No.

SUSAN. Do you see women as lesser than men?

FREDERICK. No.

SUSAN. Then do not betray us.

FREDERICK. Betray? You have no more loyal friend than I.

SUSAN. You are a coward.

FREDERICK. They are killing us!

This is not a question of rights. This is life or death for the black man.

SUSAN. For women as well.

FREDERICK. When women, because they are women, are hunted down through the streets

when their children are torn from their arms, and their brains dashed out upon the pavement

when they are in danger of having their homes burnt down over their heads

when you are dragged from your house and hung upon a lamppost

then you will have the urgency to obtain the ballot equal to my own.

SUSAN. Is that not all true about black women?

FREDERICK. Yes – it is true of the black woman – not because she is a woman, but because she is black.

SUSAN. How many women do I know – black and white – who have been beaten and raped without recourse?

Open your eyes! We cannot protect ourselves without the vote.

Our bodies are objects, constantly under attack.

If we say anything, *we* are ostracized. *We* are blamed.

It is life and death for women as well.

FREDERICK. As the child of a rape

I know of the violence women face.

SUSAN. And yet you would still do this?

FREDERICK. …Yes.

> *(His answer cuts **SUSAN** to the core.)*
>
> *(It cuts **FREDERICK** immeasurably as well.)*
>
> *(The air in the room changes – perhaps even the light does as well.)*
>
> *(They realize it will never be the same between them.)*

SUSAN. This morning, I found myself thinking of the eulogy you gave at my father's funeral.

It was beautiful.

He loved you.

FREDERICK. And I loved him.

SUSAN. And I cannot help but think – if he was alive to hear what you have said and what you are about to do – it would have broken his heart.

FREDERICK. Your father is gone. You cannot speak for him.

SUSAN. You have broken mine.

> *(She looks **FREDERICK** directly in the eyes. He looks away, unable to meet her stare.)*
>
> *(After a few moments, **FREDERICK** goes to the trunk and tries to pick it up.)*
>
> *(He fails.)*
>
> *(He closes his eyes, crouches, and tries again.)*
>
> *(With a strength that seems to come from a place he has not tapped in many years, he lifts the trunk onto his shoulder.)*
>
> *(Slowly, but steadily, he stands, bearing the immense weight on his own.)*
>
> *(Eventually, he looks **SUSAN** in the eyes.)*

End of Act One

ACT TWO

**The Commons Ball Field
City School No. 14
Rochester, New York
August 22, 1870**

*(**FREDERICK**, fifty-two years old, sits on bleachers at a baseball game.)*

(The sound of a crowd.)

(He holds a small brown bag of peanuts. He takes one out, breaks the shell, and eats it.)

FREDERICK. C'mon, now!
 C'mon, Mutuals!

(The crack of the bat.)

*(**FREDERICK** rises to his feet.)*

(He watches the flight of the ball.)

(The ball is caught. An out is recorded. He is disappointed.)

(All of the action of the ballgame occurs out over the audience, out of sight.)

 Nice try, Settle. Get 'em next time.

(He sits back down and watches intently.)

 C'mon, Mutuals!

*(After a few moments, **SUSAN**, fifty years old, enters.)*

(She wears her red shawl. She carries her alligator purse and a newspaper.)

*(She sits down in the row behind **FREDERICK**, but not far from him.)*

(They do not acknowledge each other.)

(The sound of the ball hitting the catcher's glove. A strike.)

FREDERICK. C'mon, now! Take a swing at least!

(He cracks a shell and eats a peanut.)

(To **SUSAN**.*)* I thought you did not know how to sit.

(There is another pitch. A ball.)

*(***FREDERICK*** leans back and holds the bag of peanuts out to* **SUSAN** *without looking at her.)*

(She does not take one.)

(He continues holding the bag out.)

(Eventually, he rescinds the bag. He takes one himself.)

(He breaks open the shell and eats the peanut.)

*(***SUSAN*** puts the newspaper down next to him.)*

SUSAN. What is this?

*(***FREDERICK*** glances down at the newspaper.)*

(The crack of the bat.)

(A foul ball screams toward **FREDERICK** *and* **SUSAN**.*)*

(Since he was looking down at the newspaper, **FREDERICK** *does not see the ball. He ducks out of the way and covers his head.* **SUSAN** *doesn't move or flinch.)*

(The ball flies well over their heads.)

*(***FREDERICK*** composes himself and sits back down.)*

I repeat: What is this?

FREDERICK. That looks like the most recent edition of *The New National Era*. The finest black publication in America.

*(***SUSAN*** points to a particular article.)*

SUSAN. But what is *this*?

*(**FREDERICK** shells a peanut, eats it. He looks more closely at the newspaper.)*

FREDERICK. That is an editorial about the woman suffrage movement.

SUSAN. And you wrote it?

FREDERICK. I did.

SUSAN. Is this an apology?

FREDERICK. An apology?

No.

It is the next step.

(There is a swing and a miss.)

Good swing!

Don't go down easy!

SUSAN. We have not spoken in over a year and then this?

FREDERICK. My door has been open.

SUSAN. This is one of the most brilliant arguments I have ever read in favor of women gaining the ballot.

FREDERICK. Then why do you sound upset?

SUSAN. Where was the man who wrote this last year – when we needed him?

FREDERICK. We are at a ballgame, Susan. Charles is on deck. We can talk of this another day.

SUSAN. The AERA would not have been ripped apart if –

FREDERICK. I am happy you are here. I am happy you have broken your silence to me –

but take a moment to look at the miraculous sight before us.

My son is a member of the Washington D.C. Mutuals – and here they are – playing a game against the Rochesters.

White men and black men playing baseball together.

Half the town is here. The carriages are blocking University Avenue.

A barbershop quartet is roaming about.

What a sight!

The entire team is spending the night with us tonight. It will be bedlam.

Anna insisted on staying home to prepare supper and ready the linens.

I pleaded with her to come – to no avail.

(The crack of the bat. An out is recorded.)

And now Charles is up.

(He stands.)

C'mon, Charles!

C'mon, son!

SUSAN. *(Reading from the editorial.)* "A despotism is no less a despotism because the reigning despot may be a wise and good man."

(The sound of the ball hitting the catcher's glove.)

FREDERICK. You want to talk about this now?

Fine – let us talk about this now.

(At first, he speaks his own words.)

Women cannot be represented by men.

Women must have self-definition. Self-direction. Self-representation.

(Then, he quotes **SUSAN.***)*

"No man is good enough to govern any woman without her consent."

SUSAN. Are you quoting me to me?

FREDERICK. I am.

(The crack of the bat. A foul ball.)

You and Elizabeth must be the generals. I will fall into the ranks behind you.

Any time you need me to speak – any time you need me to write an editorial – I am at your disposal.

SUSAN. You feel guilty.

FREDERICK. *No.*

I will never apologize for black men getting the right to vote.

But since it happened, I –

> *(The sound of the ball hitting the catcher's glove.)*

I see anew.

I can see that, as long as I was disenfranchised, my fight came first.

But now? I wake up in the morning and the first thing I ask myself is:

"How can I agitate today to help women gain the ballot?"

I am your soldier. There is no greater cause to me now. Would you like my help or not?

> *(**SUSAN** can hardly believe her ears.)*
>
> *(**FREDERICK** holds the bag of peanuts out to her again.)*
>
> *(Beat.)*
>
> *(She takes a peanut.)*
>
> *(The crack of the bat. A foul ball.)*
>
> *(He takes a peanut.)*
>
> *(They crack open their peanuts.)*
>
> *(They chew.)*
>
> *(**SUSAN** moves down a row and sits in the same row as **FREDERICK**.)*
>
> *(The sound of the ball hitting the catcher's glove.)*

SUSAN. How many times does the thrower throw it to Charles?

FREDERICK. Until he gets a hit – or an out – or until the balls, fouls, and strikes reach nine.

SUSAN. Then what?

FREDERICK. He would get first base on what is called a base on balls.

SUSAN. What is it now?

FREDERICK. It is at seven. No – six. The first pitch of the at bat does not count.

SUSAN. What? – why not?

> *(The crack of the bat.)*
>
> *(**FREDERICK** stands. **SUSAN** does not.)*
>
> *(They lean to the side, watching the ball fly through the air.)*

FREDERICK. Dangummit.

SUSAN. Dangummit?

FREDERICK. Dangummit.

SUSAN. Is he over with now?

FREDERICK. No, it is another foul ball.

A foul on two strikes is not a strikeout, but counts in the nine balls. And a foul is only an out if a fielder catches it on the fly or after the first bounce.

So now, he is at seven.

C'mon, Charles! C'mon, son!

> *(The crowd claps. The pitch comes...and hits Charles. They grimace.)*

SUSAN. Is he all right?

FREDERICK. It got him on the leg. He should be fine.

SUSAN. What is he doing?

FREDERICK. This is new this year – if a hitter is hit by the pitch, he goes to first.

SUSAN. But it is not nine balls yet.

FREDERICK. This trumps that rule.

SUSAN. It would seem some simplification of the rules would be helpful.

FREDERICK. Oh, they are always changing the rules.

They will get it right one of these days.

(Calling out.) C'mon, Fisher! Knock 'em home!

SUSAN. So – when shall we discuss the next steps? The plan of attack.

Do you have time tomorrow?

> *(She takes her scheduling notepad from her purse.)*

FREDERICK. The ball club has to leave on the noon train. And I –

> *(He takes out a pocket-sized notepad and checks his schedule.)*

I have to see Mayor Lutes at three.
How about one o'clock?

SUSAN. I have a committee meeting one-thirty. What about five o'clock?

FREDERICK. I have to see my editors at five.

SUSAN. How about a quarter past noon?

> *(A foul ball.)*

FREDERICK. A quarter past noon it is.

> *(They both write it down in their notepads.)*
>
> *(They get caught up in looking at their notes for other things.)*
>
> *(A historical version of getting sucked into checking their smartphones.)*
>
> *(After quite some time, **SUSAN** speaks.)*

SUSAN. Where are you off to next?

FREDERICK. I do not even know.

> *(Flipping through pages.)*

Next is…Cortland.

SUSAN. Cortland? Why?

FREDERICK. *(Checking his notes.)* For a –

> *(He stops himself.)*

SUSAN. What?

FREDERICK. …For a celebration commemorating the ratification of the Fifteenth Amendment.

> *(Beat.)*

FREDERICK. Then I must go to D.C., then Wilmington, then back to D.C. for an interview with President Grant.

SUSAN. *(Mocking how nonchalantly he said it.)* "For an interview with President Grant."

FREDERICK. And you? Where are you next?

SUSAN. Next is New York City, then lectures in Jamestown, Westfield, Bellmont, Alfred, and Corning
then New Jersey – Trenton
then back to New York – Owego, Binghamton, Elmira
then Pennsylvania – Williamsport
then Cleveland, Ohio – Aurora, Illinois – Chicago – Detroit – then D.C. – then –

FREDERICK. When are you in D.C.?

SUSAN. D.C. is...December Eighth. Will you be there?

FREDERICK. I am here in Rochester December Eighth, but back to D.C. December Fifteenth. Will you still be there?

SUSAN. No, I will be in Philadelphia.
Then lectures in Lowville, Watertown, Potsdam, Carthage –

FREDERICK. So a quarter past noon tomorrow?

SUSAN. Yes, a quarter past noon tomorrow – I have it down.

FREDERICK. On Madison Street or South Avenue?

SUSAN. Let us meet at your house. It has been too long since I have seen Anna.

FREDERICK. But it has been too long since I have seen your mother and Mary. Let us meet at yours.

SUSAN. Very well – Madison Street it is. They will be happy to see you.

FREDERICK. And I them.
(Eyeing **SUSAN**'s *purse.)* What is this bag made of?

SUSAN. Alligator.

FREDERICK. Alligator?

SUSAN. What?

FREDERICK. Now that your movement has made you famous, you galivant around the country carrying an alligator bag?

SUSAN. It is a purse. And a woman deserves a purse of her own, does she not?

FREDERICK. Yes, but –

SUSAN. This purse is a political statement. Women cannot have bank accounts. We are taxed without representation. "Every woman deserves a purse of her own."

> *(The sound of the ball hitting the catcher's glove.)*

FREDERICK. *(Calling out.)* Good eye, Fisher!
(To **SUSAN***.)* Yes, I know and I agree, but this purse is also a fashion statement.

SUSAN. This purse is a protest.
There can be no true independence for women until we are able to control our own finances.

FREDERICK. Here, here.

> *(Beat.)*

Where was the alligator from?

SUSAN. They do not tell you where the alligator is from.

FREDERICK. Mm-hm, did you ask?

SUSAN. No, but –

FREDERICK. Then perhaps it is crocodile.

SUSAN. No. It is alligator.

> *(They look at the purse, trying to discern its origins.)*

FREDERICK. Speaking of reptiles, how is Mr. Train?

SUSAN. It has been more than a year since we parted ways.

FREDERICK. Remind me – why did you part ways?
Because he is a racist?
Or because he stopped sending checks?

SUSAN. Frederick –

FREDERICK. Which was it?

SUSAN. ...Both.

FREDERICK. Mm-hm.

(They watch the game in silence for a moment.)

SUSAN. *(Yelling out.)* C'mon! Throw the ball instead of merely talking about throwing the ball!

(To **FREDERICK**.*)* What is this? The man catching the ball can go speak with the man throwing the ball for as long as he wishes? How long will this game last?

(Yelling out.) Enough with this tomfoolery! Throw it – dangummit!

*(**FREDERICK** looks at **SUSAN**, surprised.)*

(He laughs.)

FREDERICK. We still know how to surprise each other.

SUSAN. Indeed.

*(She reaches over and gently squeezes **FREDERICK**'s hand.)*

(He pulls away.)

What?

FREDERICK. *(Quietly.)* There is a white man – red in the face – staring at us.

He clearly does not think we make a suitable pairing.

*(**SUSAN** looks.)*

Do not look at him.

SUSAN. Pay him no attention.

FREDERICK. He has a pistol in his pocket. I saw it glimmer in the sunlight.

(Beat.)

He does not look this way at the black man selling peanuts to the white woman.

He hates me, not because I am black, but because we are talking as equals. Because you and I are friends.

SUSAN. He is talking to a police officer. Dear Lord –

FREDERICK. Never touch me in public again.

Now I must miss my son's game.

(He starts to leave.)

SUSAN. You are going to leave me here alone to face them?
FREDERICK. Your skin will keep you safe.

(He exits.)

*(Stunned, **SUSAN** watches him go.)*

(She looks toward the man and the police officer. She stands.)

(The barbershop quartet begins to sing "Shoo Fly, Don't Bother Me.")

*(After several moments, **SUSAN** leaves.)*

(A spark flies through the air.)

(Another.)

(A fire begins to burn.)

(The quartet continues to sing the song's original, racist lyrics.)

(The flames flicker.)

(Smoke fills the air.)

(The wood snaps.)

(The fire grows and grows.)

(The roar of the heat can be heard, but over it we can still hear the hateful song.)

(The fire engulfs all.)

The Douglass House
South Avenue, Rochester, New York
June 5, 1872

(It is almost two years later.)
(The burnt remains of Frederick's house.)
(There are the scarred black skeletons of trees.)
(The ground smolders.)

(It rains.)

(A flash of lightning. A low rumble of thunder in the distance.)

*(**SUSAN**, now fifty-two years old, holds her umbrella above both her and **FREDERICK**, now fifty-four years old.)*

(They look out over the destruction.)

FREDERICK. When I received word that my house burnt down, my first thought was:

I am surprised it did not happen sooner.

   (Beat.)

I left D.C. in such a rush, I did not think to bring an umbrella.

Why would I bring an umbrella to a fire?

   (Beat.)

Thank the Lord no one was hurt.

I implored Anna to stay away. This destruction is too much for her to bear.

…Even in the North, the property of the colored man is less respected and less secure than the property of any white citizen.

SUSAN. They have not yet identified the cause.

FREDERICK. There is no question of who did this. And why.

SUSAN. The police are not yet calling it arson.

FREDERICK. They can call it whatever they please.

My time here is through.

Washington, D.C. will be my home now.

SUSAN. Please do not say that.

FREDERICK. It is the Ku Klux spirit that lit this match.

SUSAN. But this is Rochester.

FREDERICK. Indeed – but even though Rochester is among the most liberal of Northern cities, there is still hatred. Whether it is out in the open or boiling below.

SUSAN. Please wait until the investigation is over before you –

FREDERICK. There does not need to be an investigation. Can you not see what is smoldering before you?

SUSAN. Yes, but –

FREDERICK. This is arson. This is hate. I have been enduring it my entire life and so this comes as no surprise. But what pains me more so than whoever did this – is that you, one of my oldest friends, do not immediately condemn this act as arson and hate.

>   *(Beat.)*

What is it that keeps driving us apart?
Is it the Fifteenth Amendment?
Is it an angry mob? An angry man at a baseball game?
Is it whoever lit this match?
It always seems to be someone else – somewhere else – but what if –
What if it is right here between us?

SUSAN. Frederick, I feel a pain in my chest as though my own house burnt down.

FREDERICK. But your house was not burnt down.
Mine was.
...We are standing here
the two of us
who love one another –
we are looking at the same thing
and yet, we see two different realities.

SUSAN. ...I do not want to believe my city is capable of this.
I do not want you to leave.
I do not want to lose my friend.

FREDERICK. Do you still believe this can be a country for all?

SUSAN. Yes.

FREDERICK. Then look at what is before you
and try to see what I see.

(Beat.)

*(**SUSAN** tries to look anew.)*

SUSAN. ...I see the skeletons of trees
you planted some twenty-five years ago.
I see Anna's lilacs
turned to ash.
And if I look up and down the road, I see that no other property has so much as a flower out of place.
This is the work of an incendiary
of a hate-filled person
who wishes to drive away Rochester's most beloved son.
Do not let them win.
Please do not leave.

FREDERICK. There is nothing left for me here.

(He starts to leave.)

(He sees something.)

(He reaches into the burnt remains and pulls out his violin case.)

(He takes a deep breath and opens the case.)

(The violin is in perfect condition. There is not so much as a scratch on it.)

(He takes out the violin. He takes the bow.)

...Will you give me a moment?

*(**SUSAN** nods.)*

(She exits.)

*(**FREDERICK** readies his violin. He closes his eyes.)*

(For a moment, the sound of children playing.)

(He plays something new.)

(He plays a melody he has never heard or played before.)

(It is a eulogy for the house and the memories in it.)

(Time passes.)
(He continues to play.)
(There is a cold gust of wind.)
(Snow begins to fall.)
(The snow covers the burnt remains of the house.)
(He attacks the strings of his violin anew.)
(The melody soars.)
(The door of a new house rises.)
(The music is triumphant.)
(Suddenly, he plays an abrupt, violent interval.)
(His song quickly descends into anguish and despair.)
(He falls to his knees.)

The Douglass House
Cedar Hill, Washington, D.C.
January 21, 1883

(It is ten and a half years later.)
*(**FREDERICK**, now sixty-four years old, kneels on the floor, shivering.)*

SUSAN. *(Offstage.)* Frederick!

(The sound of knocking on the door.)

Frederick, the door is wide open. Are you there?

(More knocking.)

I am coming in!
It is Susan and I am coming in!

*(After a moment, **SUSAN**, now sixty-two years old, enters the living room.)*
(She wears a winter coat and hat.)

(She carries her alligator purse.)

*(She sees **FREDERICK**.)*

SUSAN. Frederick, why did you leave the door open?
It is freezing in here.
Let me put on the fire.

(She immediately starts the fire in the stove.)

FREDERICK. Fire is not welcome in this house.

SUSAN. You will catch pneumonia otherwise.

FREDERICK. I welcome the cold.
Why are you here?

SUSAN. To see you.

FREDERICK. Why are you in D.C.?

SUSAN. For the National. Our convention begins tomorrow.

FREDERICK. I am in no condition to speak this year. If that is why you are here, I –

SUSAN. That is not why I am here.

FREDERICK. I cannot give any lectures!

SUSAN. I do not expect you to.
Is anyone here?

FREDERICK. No. Charles visited the other day with Joseph.
Have you met my grandson Joseph?

SUSAN. Yes, of course.

FREDERICK. Has he played violin for you?

SUSAN. No, not yet.

FREDERICK. He is twelve and already playing Mozart and Mendelssohn.
He already plays better than his grandfather. But he is not yet better than his grandmother.
He has the makings of a virtuoso.
He loved it when Anna and I played on the porch together.
Children came from all over the neighborhood to listen to our duets.

*(**SUSAN** puts more wood in the stove.)*

The warmth is…
Thank you.
I lost track of time. On the porch.

> *(Beat.)*

Time has been behaving so strangely since Anna died.

> *(Beat.)*

How do you clean grease from a suit coat?

SUSAN. …Cover the stain with talcum powder. Let it set for a half hour.
Then, using a little bit of water, gently wash it out with your hands.

FREDERICK. Ah.

SUSAN. Before I forget…

> *(She goes to her alligator purse and takes out a thick, leather-bound book.)*

For you.

FREDERICK. Bravo.
(Reading.) "*History of Woman Suffrage: Volume Two.* Edited by Elizabeth Cady Stanton, Susan B. Anthony, and Matilda Joslyn Gage."
Why not list your names alphabetically?
Why Elizabeth first?

SUSAN. Oh, we are all first. And many, many more women than the three of us.
If we could list a thousand names, all first, we would.

FREDERICK. I look forward to reading it.

SUSAN. I did not send it earlier because I was waiting for the leather-bound edition. I could not give Frederick Douglass a cloth-bound copy – no.

FREDERICK. Thank you.

SUSAN. What did you think of the first volume? I do not believe we ever spoke about it.

FREDERICK. I…love the beginning. A very strong beginning. Which, of course, is so important.

(Beat.)

SUSAN. You did not read it.

FREDERICK. I read the first chapter and it was very strong.

SUSAN. But not strong enough to keep reading?

FREDERICK. I will finish it. I promise.

And I look forward to volume two.

(Beat.)

Let me get you a copy of my third autobiography.

SUSAN. I already have one.

FREDERICK. And?

SUSAN. ...And I look forward to reading it.

*(**FREDERICK** laughs. **SUSAN** laughs.)*

*(**FREDERICK** steels himself and looks at the fire.)*

(They both watch the fire in silence.)

*(After some time, **FREDERICK** speaks.)*

FREDERICK. Once I saw infinite light.

Have you ever?

*(Beat. **SUSAN** doesn't know how to answer.)*

I saw the constancy of hate break down
and the clouds of pride and selfishness vanish
before a brightness of infinite light.

(Beat.)

When I was away on my lecturing tours, Anna would send fresh linens for me – ahead of my arrival. Those towels and sheets smelled of her.

Of her hands.

Her skin.

I never had trouble falling asleep away from home because of her linens.

What will I do without her?

SUSAN. Anna is still with you.

FREDERICK. She allowed me to focus entirely on agitation.

She thought of every detail imaginable.

Anna Murray-Douglass allowed me to be Frederick Douglass.

But she gave too much. She gave everything.

…She was a much better wife to me than I was a husband to her.

I have been sleeping on the floor.

It is the only way I can fall asleep now.

Have you ever slept on the floor?

SUSAN. …No.

FREDERICK. I did not sleep in a bed until I was twenty years old – and now, without her, I…

Try it. Lie down.

SUSAN. I am not going to lie on your floor.

FREDERICK. Well, I am. I must.

>*(He lies down on the floor. He takes off his shoes.)*
>
>*(After several moments,* **SUSAN** *lies down on the floor as well.)*
>
>*(They stare at the ceiling.)*
>
>*(The light from the fireplace flickers.)*
>
>*(A long time passes.)*

Would you like a pillow?

SUSAN. No, thank you.

FREDERICK. I am going to use a pillow.

>*(He takes the book and puts it under his head.)*

…The floor and the *History of Woman Suffrage: Volume Two* under my head.

What more could a modern man possibly need?

>*(He laughs.)*
>
>*(***SUSAN*** laughs.)*
>
>*(He begins to cry.)*

How have you done it? All these years?

SUSAN. Done what?

FREDERICK. Been on your own.

SUSAN. I am not on my own. I have my sister in the house with me. I had my mother until three years ago. I am not on my own.

FREDERICK. How have you traversed through life without sharing your heart?

SUSAN. I share my heart every time I open my mouth.

And besides, a woman is not incomplete without a husband.

I am not a half. I am whole.

FREDERICK. I do not need Susan B. Anthony right now – I need Susan.

I need the help of one of my dearest friends left alive.

How am I going to survive this?

How have you not shared your heart with a lover? How?

SUSAN. ...I have.

FREDERICK. Who?

(Pause.)

SUSAN. I am married to the Cause.

FREDERICK. But you cannot hear the Cause breathing next to you. The Cause cannot caress you and hold you and kiss your neck.

SUSAN. I wake up thinking of it. I spend every minute of every day devoted to it.

I go to sleep – thinking of the problems we are facing – and I wake up with answers.

Or possible answers. I am so embraced by it, and it by me, that now I dream of it.

And when I think of these fine young women around me – so dedicated to amending the Constitution, I –

FREDERICK. But have you ever fallen in love?

SUSAN. ...Yes.

FREDERICK. With who?

> (**SUSAN** *does not answer. A long pause.*)

SUSAN. ...When I cannot fall asleep, I breathe in through my nose and out from my mouth.

Try it.

In with your nose.

> (*Still lying on the floor, they both breathe in through their noses.*)

Out from your mouth.

> (*They breathe out from their mouths.*)

In.

> (*They breathe in.*)

Out.

> (*They breathe out.*)

FREDERICK. What am I going to do?

> (*They breathe in.*)
>
> (*They breathe out.*)

SUSAN. (*Quietly.*) ...A rich man took up his residence next to a tanner.

And the rich man found the smell of the tanyard so unpleasant that he told the tanner he must go.

The tanner kept delaying his departure.

The rich man spoke to him over and over.

And every time the tanner said, "I am making the arrangements to move very soon."

This back and forth went on for some time, till at last the rich man got so used to the smell that he ceased to mind it, and he troubled the tanner with objections no more.

...In.

> (*They breathe in.*)

Out.

> (*They breathe out.*)

(From far away in the distance, the sound of a brass band playing a march.* Perhaps it is Johann Strauss I's "Radetzky March.")

The White House
Washington, D.C.
March 30, 1888

(It is five years later.)

(SUSAN and FREDERICK lie on their backs on the main corridor of the White House.)

(SUSAN, now sixty-eight, and FREDERICK, seventy, look up at the ceiling.)

(FREDERICK still has a thick book under his head.)

(The Marine Band finishes the march with a flourish.)

FREDERICK. *(Pointing.)* There.

You see the gold leaf there – where the new traceries are. Indeed – they spell "U.S.A."

SUSAN. Where?

FREDERICK. U. S. A.

You see?

SUSAN. No.

Why am I even here? President Cleveland has done nothing to help the women's cause.

FREDERICK. Enjoy it! It is an accomplishment to be invited to the White House.

SUSAN. It is not an accomplishment if it accomplishes nothing.

**A license to produce *The Agitators* does not include a performance license for any third-party or copyrighted music. Licensees should create an original composition or use music in the public domain. For further information, please see Music Use Note on page 3.

I tried to speak to him of our continued disenfranchisement – Princess Viroqua tried to speak to him of her plans for an Indian college – but all he wanted to talk about was the new traceries on the ceiling in the main corridor.

And I do not see the hidden letters.

Why are your shoes off?

FREDERICK. Grover told us to make ourselves comfortable.

SUSAN. Frederick Douglass, put your shoes back on.

FREDERICK. Here. Try propping the *History of Woman Suffrage: Volume Three* under your head.

>*(He props the book under **SUSAN**'s head.)*
>
>*(He starts to put his shoes back on.)*

I still cannot believe you brought me volume three today.

SUSAN. Once the International Council begins, I was afraid I would forget.

FREDERICK. It has proved quite useful to place *hors d'oeuvres* on.

SUSAN. How did you like volumes one and two?

FREDERICK. They...

SUSAN. Have excellent first chapters?

FREDERICK. Yes. Quite excellent.

SUSAN. Oh.

I see a U.

An S.

An A.

Rah rah sis boom bah.

Enough of this lounging.

>*(**SUSAN**, defying her age, springs to her feet.)*

FREDERICK. How did you do that?

>*(**SUSAN** offers him her hand. He takes it. His getting up is not an easy process. He lets out several strained sounds. Eventually, he makes it up. She hands him the book.)*

SUSAN. *(Looking down the hall.)* The First Lady is scowling at us.

I told you we should not lie down in the hallway.

FREDERICK. Oh, that is not why she is scowling at you.

SUSAN. I beg your pardon?

FREDERICK. In the receiving line, as you introduced your pioneers to the President, one after another, making him laugh and smile – you never once lifted your hand from his shoulder. I daresay, at times, you were caressing him.

Mrs. Cleveland was green with envy.

SUSAN. You are imagining things.

FREDERICK. Everyone in the East Room noticed, Susan – even the reporter from *The Washington Post*.

You must take care. Frances is our youngest First Lady ever and prone to jealousy.

*(**SUSAN** looks down the hall, sticks her tongue out, and blows a raspberry at the First Lady.)*

SUSAN. How old is she?

FREDERICK. Twenty-three.

SUSAN. And how old is he?

FREDERICK. Fifty-one.

SUSAN. Twenty-eight years her senior?

It is reprehensi–

(She stops herself. Beat.)

FREDERICK. Helen is only twenty years younger than me. Why would I take offense?

...She thinks you do not like her.

SUSAN. I like Helen.

FREDERICK. You take no interest in her. You have barely spoken to her today.

SUSAN. Well, apparently, I have been too preoccupied flirting with the President.

FREDERICK. I was lost. She brought light back into my life.

SUSAN. I can see that.

FREDERICK. She thinks you do not approve of our marriage.

SUSAN. On what grounds?

FREDERICK. That she is twenty years younger than me.

That she was my secretary.

That she is white.

Elizabeth publicly supported our marriage.

SUSAN. You want me to write a letter and publish it like Elizabeth did?

My concern is votes for women and nothing else.

I am not concerned with the age of your wife or the color of her skin.

Now it is time for me to leave this pointless affair – and get back to work.

FREDERICK. Please stay.

SUSAN. Stay for what? This ceremony is the only thing this administration has ever done for the women's cause.

(Yelling down the hall.) And I could make a better butternut squash confit with my eyes closed!

(To **FREDERICK.***)* You have been in Washington, D.C. too long, Frederick.

You have become a politician – jockeying for useless, pointless posts.

You live up high on Cedar Hill, in a house with twenty-one rooms.

Where is the man who told me to agitate, agitate, agitate?

And I know – you are seventy years old.

I know you have already done so much good – I should leave you alone.

But I will not.

We need you.

The Negroes being lynched in the South need you – and those being illegally disenfranchised at the polls.

The women who still have no vote need you.

The International Council convenes tomorrow night.
We have fifty-three women's associations here from nine different countries.

Come speak.

Come share your thunder and lightning – if you have any left.

> *(She exits, leaves the White House.)*
>
> *(**FREDERICK** stands there, stunned.)*
>
> *(The Marine Band begins playing "Hail to the Chief.")*
>
> *(**FREDERICK** turns to a mirror. He looks at himself.)*
>
> *(He breathes in through his nose.)*
>
> *(He breathes out through his mouth.)*

The Anthony House
17 Madison Street, Rochester, New York
December 23, 1894

> *(It is six and a half years later. The front room of Susan's house.)*
>
> *(It is a cold, blustery Rochester winter morning.)*
>
> *(**FREDERICK**, now seventy-six years old, waits. He looks at a scrapbook of photographs and newspaper articles.)*
>
> *(On the chair next to him rests his cane, his wool overcoat, and his fur hat.)*
>
> *(He hums the same four notes from the beginning of the play.)*
>
> *(He cannot remember any more of it.)*
>
> *(**SUSAN**, now seventy-four years old, enters with a present behind her back.)*
>
> *(For a moment, **FREDERICK** doesn't notice her.)*

(He hums the first four notes again.)

SUSAN. ...Have you found your mother's song?

FREDERICK. ...Not yet.

> *(**SUSAN** takes the present from behind her back. It is wrapped in brown paper. It has yarn or a festive ribbon wrapped around it.)*

What is this?

SUSAN. A present.

FREDERICK. Quakers do not celebrate Christmas.

SUSAN. But you do.

> *(**FREDERICK** pulls the yarn or ribbon from the gift.)*
>
> *(He takes off the brown paper. He opens the lid of the box.)*
>
> *(He takes out a pair of ice skates. He is at a loss.)*

FREDERICK. Ice skates?

SUSAN. Ice skates!

FREDERICK. Did you give me the wrong box?

SUSAN. I thought we might go ice skate on the Genesee River. The river being frozen over is the one good thing about winter here.

FREDERICK. I do not know how to ice skate.

SUSAN. Would you like to learn? – after Mary returns from the market?

FREDERICK. Thank you, Susan, but as enticing of an offer as this is –
to learn how to ice skate at the age of seventy-six
with two sisters – who are also in their seventies
on a frozen river –
I think I will pass.
I am here, after all, for a funeral.

SUSAN. ...Perhaps another time.

FREDERICK. *(Nope, no way, never.)* Perhaps.

SUSAN. How is Helen doing?

FREDERICK. As well as she can be.

SUSAN. My condolences.

I am glad Helen could make it here to attend her aunt's funeral in Honeoye.

...I knew Helen's family did not approve of your marriage, but this is –

FREDERICK. I knew our lives together would be full of moments like this.

SUSAN. You are one of the greatest men of the nineteenth century and yet you are not welcome at the funeral? It is deplorable.

FREDERICK. While I wish I could be there, I am grateful to be here.

> *(He points to the headline of the article he was reading in the scrapbook.)*

(Proudly.) "Susan B. Anthony Arrested for Voting Illegally."

I forgot that you demanded to be handcuffed.

SUSAN. I most certainly did. I demanded to be treated no differently than a man.

FREDERICK. You caused quite a stir.

SUSAN. That was more than a stir. It was in the headlines across the country for the better part of a year.

FREDERICK. And it happened right here at 17 Madison Street.

SUSAN. To think – one time in our lives – we both voted:

On November the Fifth, 1872, you and I cast our ballots for President Grant.

If only both of our actions were legal.

FREDERICK. ...How long ago did we meet?

SUSAN. More than forty-five years ago now.

FREDERICK. Hard to believe.

SUSAN. Indeed.

FREDERICK. Feels more like fifty-five or sixty.

> *(Beat.)*

Here – let us sit.

SUSAN. I am fine standing.

FREDERICK. Good Lord, woman – sit!

I have seen you sit two or three times in my life.

(SUSAN remains standing.)

How are your feet?

SUSAN. Throbbing with stabbing, sharp pains – like a thousand little needles piercing.

FREDERICK. Please sit.

SUSAN. I am used to it.

FREDERICK. Susan –

SUSAN. I do not know how to sit.

FREDERICK. Well, I do.

(Beat. He sits down.)

(SUSAN remains standing. She begins to pace.)

Will you be here in Rochester on April the Seventh?

SUSAN. April the Seventh is a…Sunday.

I must be in Chicago on April First and in Sodus for a lecture on the Tenth.

I will be here, yes.

FREDERICK. Ida B. Wells has been invited by the black leaders here in Rochester to give a series of lectures. I can make it here on the Seventh.

Have you heard her speak yet?

SUSAN. No.

FREDERICK. Will you go with me?

SUSAN. Yes, of course.

FREDERICK. You opened my eyes at the White House so many years ago, but it is Ida B. Wells who has awakened my soul.

(SUSAN begins to pace more quickly.)

Her investigative journalism on lynchings has caused a great agitation. Most people in the North have no idea of the prejudice and terror that continues now in the South.

Miss Wells is –

Why are you pacing?

SUSAN. There is a business matter I must discuss with you.

(Beat.)

You know it was not my wish to have the National Convention in Atlanta next month. I believe it should always be in D.C., where we are in arm's length of Congress and can easily pull on their ears.

FREDERICK. You have made that clear.

But I believe there is a great good to accomplish in Atlanta.

SUSAN. ...You know that the National does not have any jurisdiction over local chapters' restrictions on membership.

(Beat. She sits.)

The Georgia Chapter has decided to prohibit black women from attending the convention.

(Beat.)

This is why I did not want to have the convention in the South.

FREDERICK. Let us invite the black women anyway. Let us take the fight to them.

SUSAN. There are millions of white, Southern women who have yet to join the movement. With their support and financial backing, with them convincing their husbands to vote for woman suffrage, it could turn the tide in this fight.

FREDERICK. Yes, but –

SUSAN. The local officers explicitly said, if colored women were at the convention, their white constituents would not attend.

I hate this. But the convention only lasts six days – and it could make the difference in whether or not we pass the amendment that will enfranchise *all* women in this country forever.

FREDERICK. Then let me speak. I was not planning on going to Atlanta, but I can speak on the matter of this so-called Negro problem.

SUSAN. Our cause is votes for women. We cannot make the fight about anything else.

You do not need to come to Atlanta.

FREDERICK. How many times have you begged me to speak?

SUSAN. I have not begged.

FREDERICK. Strongly urged.

Implored.

Insisted.

Well, now I am begging you. Let me speak.

(With his old thunder and lightning.) "Men talk of the Negro problem.

There is no Negro problem.

The problem is whether the American people have loyalty enough,

honor enough,

patriotism enough

to live up to their own Constitution."

Let me speak.

SUSAN. No.

> *(Beat.* **FREDERICK** *picks up one of the ice skates by the blade.)*

FREDERICK. You misremembered the story, Susan. It was not I who wanted to ice skate, but my daughter Annie.

SUSAN. I know. I only thought that –

FREDERICK. "Fight for my rights, Aunt Susan."

"Fight for my rights."

When did you stop fighting for little Annie?

SUSAN. I am still fighting for her.

FREDERICK. But if she was still alive she could not attend this convention.

SUSAN. I did not want the convention in Atlanta!

FREDERICK. Then have it in D.C. instead.

SUSAN. It is too late to move it to D.C.

FREDERICK. Then cancel it.

SUSAN. It is too late to cancel it.

FREDERICK. Where is the woman who thrust out her wrists and said, "Handcuff me!"?

SUSAN. It is not the right time.

FREDERICK. It is always the right time to speak out against injustice!

> *(Without thinking, he squeezes the blade of an ice skate.)*
>
> *(He cuts the palm of his hand.)*
>
> *(Blood pours out.)*

Dammit.

SUSAN. Let us get you a doctor.

> *(**FREDERICK** takes out his handkerchief and wraps his hand in it.)*

FREDERICK. There is no need.

SUSAN. Your hand is cut open.

FREDERICK. I have been cut much worse.

> *(He grabs his coat.)*

SUSAN. Please do not leave.

FREDERICK. I think I must.

> *(He goes to the door and opens it. Snow blows inside.)*
>
> *(He is about to leave, but instead he stands in the doorframe.)*
>
> *(He lifts his hands above his head and pushes upward against the doorframe.)*
>
> *(The handkerchief around his hand is now red.)*

The oak tree said to the reeds,

"How have you weathered the storm, whereas I have been torn up by the roots and hurled into the river?"

"You were stubborn," said the reeds, "and the storm proved stronger than you. But we reeds, we bow and yield to every breeze, and the gale passed harmlessly over our heads."

> *(He slowly lowers his arms.)*
>
> *(He lets a cold gust of wind from outside pass through him.)*
>
> *(He steps back inside. He calmly closes the door.)*
>
> *(He faces* **SUSAN**.*)*

Earlier this year, you went to all sixty counties in New York in three months – did you not?

SUSAN. Yes.

FREDERICK. Sixty counties in three months – at the age of seventy-four.

In Wyoming and Colorado, women can vote in local elections.

The National's membership is larger than ever before.

Perhaps what you are doing is working.

SUSAN. It is.

FREDERICK. You are the most famous woman in America.

Perhaps in all the world.

SUSAN. Queen Victoria is the most famous woman in the world.

FREDERICK. Then you are second to her.

People listen to you. Why sacrifice your ideals now?

SUSAN. I am not sacrificing my ideals. This is a compromise.

FREDERICK. This is staying silent in the face of a grave injustice.

SUSAN. Were you not sacrificing your ideals in 1869? When you abandoned the women's cause?

FREDERICK. I did not abandon it.

SUSAN. Nor am I abandoning black women now.

Our ideals are the same – they always have been.

FREDERICK. Remind me?

SUSAN. To make this into a country for All.

FREDERICK. Then why do we keep having the same fight over and over?

SUSAN. You did not apologize to me then.

I will not apologize to you now.

We disagree on strategy.

We did over the Fifteenth Amendment.

We do today.

FREDERICK. In 1869, I did what I did because I thought:

This hateful, hypocritical country is not ready for equality all at once.

We must get it piece by piece.

I thought:

The language of the Fifteenth *is* flawed

but it is what we can get.

We, the disenfranchised.

And the only reason I –

the only reason I sacrificed my ideals

is I thought you were right behind us.

I thought:

Women will secure the vote in four or five years – at worst, it will take ten years.

That was twenty-four years ago.

I thought you were right behind us, but it has been twenty-four years.

Susan, if you sacrifice your ideals for six days –

if you step on others to get what you want –

SUSAN. Frederick –

FREDERICK. If you do this – it will cost you.

You may not feel it next week or next year

but it will eat away at you like a cancer.

I was not prepared for the cost.

And I say this to you – not out of malice – but as your dearest friend.

Do not do this.

SUSAN. …My whole life I have been told to wait.

I present petitions to, literally, the grandsons of the congressmen I first presented petitions to.

From the day we are born, we women are pushed aside.

We are told that our voices do not matter.

That we are not citizens.

That we are lesser.

This

sacrifice

could lead to the enfranchisement of *all* women.

If you want crops, you must plow the ground.

The convention must go on.

(They look at one another for several moments.)

*(Eventually, **FREDERICK** lowers his head.)*

FREDERICK. Lord –

Will you, one day, give us the strength

to fight for each other

as much as we fight for ourselves?

And until that day,

will you please have mercy on our souls?

Until that day,

will you give us the strength to forgive one another?

And to forgive ourselves.

Amen.

SUSAN. Amen.

FREDERICK. …I will make the trip here in April to hear Ida B. Wells.

I hope you will join me.

SUSAN. I will.

FREDERICK. Her last speech still echoes in my head. It burned into my memory when I heard it:

"I long with all the intensity of my soul that mob rule shall be put down

and equal justice be accorded to every citizen of this country –

no matter the race –

when every member of this great composite nation will be a living, harmonious illustration of the *words*:

> *(He speaks the lyrics.)*

My country, 'tis of thee,
Sweet land of liberty

> *(The light in the front room grows brighter and brighter.)*

Of thee I sing.
Land where our fathers died,
Land of the Pilgrims' pride,
From every mountainside –"

> *(The front room fills with infinite light. Nothing else can be seen.)*

Mount Hope Cemetery
Rochester, New York
April 11, 1895

(It is three months later.)

(A beautiful, spring morning.)

(Birds chirp. A pleasant breeze comes and goes.)

*(**SUSAN**, now seventy-five years old, enters.)*

(She wears her red shawl. She carries her alligator purse.)

(She goes to a grave.)

(Throughout the speech, she remains standing. She stays front-footed, searching for answers. She resists any kind of sentimentality.)

SUSAN. Frederick, I wanted to tell you who is staying at our house now – at this very moment.

Tomorrow, she will take the train back to Memphis. But today, she is here in Rochester and a guest at 17 Madison Street.

(Beat.)

Miss Ida B. Wells.

You were right about her.

I went to her lecture at First Baptist Church and she – she has lightning in her eyes and thunder in her words.

After the lecture, I met Miss Wells.

And she was...quite critical of me.

She appreciated that I spoke out against discrimination in the North, but she does not understand why I seem to accept it in the South.

Why I accepted it in Atlanta.

"I refuse to compromise on issues of black rights," she said. "And you should refuse to as well."

I then invited her to stay with us for the rest of her time in Rochester.

"I was afraid I put you off," she said.

But I told her, "It is the trait I most desire in my friends."

We have had an extraordinary time.

Until yesterday.

I had to go to Sodus to give a lecture. In the morning, I told Miss Wells she could use my new stenographer for her correspondence.

I did not know this young woman well. Anna Dorsey. I only knew – she was twenty years old. She was destitute and desperately needed the work. And she could type well enough.

When I returned home last night, I found Miss Wells scribbling away by herself and the stenographer at leisure.

I asked her, "Why is Miss Wells doing her own letters and not you?"

And she plainly said, without any remorse, "I do not write letters for any colored person."

And I replied, "If you cannot oblige me by assisting a guest in my house, you cannot remain in my employ."

And this young woman, who has no home and not a penny to her name, left without another word.

I was stunned.

I played the scene out over and over.

What would you have done, Frederick?

Should I not have given her this ultimatum?

How could I have done a better job at helping her see?

But I gave her a choice – and she decided she would rather starve to death than be subservient to a black woman.

And I decided that I could not have that hatred in my house.

(Beat.)

If these United States are ever to be truly united –
How can we learn to stay in the room
with the people we hate? –
and who hate us.
How can we be better at helping each other see?
...There is so much work to be done
and the thought of doing it without you is –

(Beat.)

But then I think of the young people around us –
Anna Howard Shaw
Fannie Barrier Williams
Booker T. Washington
Rachel Foster Avery
Ida B. Wells –
the list goes on and on –

when I think of these fine, young agitators – and the countless ones who are not yet born, I –
Failure is impossible.

> *(Beat.)*

I finally heard your grandson Joseph play violin.
It was in D.C. at a Waller's Benefit concert.
And when he began to play, I could scarcely believe my ears.
He played the song you have tried to find all these years.
It was unmistakable.

> *(She hums the first four notes.)*

The Mendelssohn Violin Concerto.
What if – all this time – you were not hearing the past, but the song of what is to come?

> *(The opening notes of Mendelssohn's "Violin Concerto in E Minor" ring out.)*
>
> *(It begins with the first four notes we have heard many times before.)*
>
> *(In the distance, we see the silhouette of a violinist.)*
>
> *(He is a tall, young black man.)*
>
> *(He plays the violin. He sways freely to the music.)*
>
> *(**SUSAN** looks at Frederick's grave.)*
>
> *(She looks at where her own grave will be.)*
>
> *(The symphony swells beneath the violinist.)*
>
> *(**SUSAN** turns to listen, rapt.)*

End of Play

www.ingramcontent.com/pod-product-compliance
Lightning Source LLC
Chambersburg PA
CBHW051409290426
44108CB00015B/2212